VIRGINIA IS A COUNTRY OF *AMERICA*, that lyeth betweene the degrees of 34 and 44 of the north latitude. The bounds thereof on the East side are the great *Ocean*. On the South, lyeth *Florida*: on the North *nova Francia*. As for the West thereof, the limits are vnknowne.

—CAPT. JOHN SMITH, "DESCRIPTION OF VIRGINIA," 1612

(Page 1, overleaf) DISMAL SWAMP. The swamp presented a formidable obstacle to colonial planter William Byrd II when he was commissioned to survey the dividing line between Virginia and North Carolina in 1728. "Tis hardly credible how little the Bordering inhabitants were acquainted with this mighty Swamp, notwithstanding they had liv'd their whole lives within Smell of it. Yet, as great Strangers as they were to it, they pretended to be very exact in their Account of its Dimensions, and were positive it could not be above 7 or 8 miles wide, but knew no more of the Matter than Star-gazers know of the Distance of the Fixt Stars. At the same time, they were Simple enough to amuse our Men with Idle Stories of the Lyons, Panthers and Alligators they were like to encounter in that dreadful Place. In short, we saw plainly there was no Intelligence of this Terra Incognita to be got, but from our own Experience." Byrd nearly lost his surveying party in the morass. Out of provisions, exhausted, and feverish from the damp, his men emerged from the swamp after nine anxious days.

(Pages 2-3, overleaf) SUSAN CONSTANT, GODSPEED, AND *DISCOVERY*. Replicas of the sailing ships that brought the 105 colonists from England in 1607 are anchored at Jamestown Festival Park, near the marshy island in the James River where the first permanent English-speaking settlement in the New World was founded. "James Towne" was decimated by disease and famine. The colony survived, however, and the House of Burgesses, the first representative legislature in America, convened there in 1619.

(Pages 4-5, overleaf) EASTERN SHORE. A 70-mile long peninsula bordered on one side by the Atlantic Ocean and on the other by Chesapeake Bay, the Eastern Shore is laced with hundreds of streams. Its marshlands are home to a variety of wildfowl, including ducks, geese, bitterns, herons, egrets, ospreys, and bald eagles.

(Pages 6-7, overleaf) ALLEGHENY MOUNTAINS. "It is worthy notice," wrote Thomas Jefferson in his *Notes on the State of Virginia*, "that our mountains are not solitary and scattered confusedly over the face of the country; but that they commence at about 150 miles from the sea-coast, are disposed in ridges one behind another, running nearly parallel with the sea-coast, though rather approaching it as they advance north-eastwardly....the courses of the great rivers are at right angles with these. James and Patowmac penetrate through all the ridges of mountains eastward of the Alleghaney, that is broken by no water course. It is in fact the spine of the country between the Atlantic on one side, and the Missisipi and St. Laurence on the other."

WOODLANDS. Timber has been Virginia's most constant export. Captain Christopher Newport in 1607 took back oak timber to be made into ships' masts. Lumber played an important role in the Virginia economy during Reconstruction. While the giant cypresses of Southside and the massive chestnut trees of the mountains have largely disappeared, planting programs are helping to preserve Virginia's timber resources.

Library of Congress catalog number 84-052617
ISBN 0-934738-12-2
Printed and bound in Japan by Dai Nippon Printing Co., Ltd.
Any inquiries should be directed to the publisher, Thomasson, Grant & Howell, Inc.,
2250-6 Old Ivy Road, Charlottesville, Virginia 22901.
Compiled and edited by Ross A. Howell, Jr.
Designed by John F. Grant and Marilyn F. Appleby.
Produced by Frank L. Thomasson, III.

THOMASSON, GRANT & HOWELL

VIRGINIA
AN AERIAL PORTRAIT

PHOTOGRAPHY BY ROBERT LLEWELLYN

THE PHOTOGRAPHS in these pages are a portrait of Virginia. They show what's been done with the land and the waters; how the state has changed, and is changing; how the wilderness remains. On another level, the photographs are a self-portrait. They say something about the photographer. When you look at the images, perhaps you will learn something about me, about the subject, and about yourself. Exploration is synonymous with growth. I feel a need to grow — to discover and understand new things.

As a photographer, I find myself searching for the special moment when I am able to bring together skill, concentration, light, image, and equipment to record beauty and peace — perhaps "grace" is a better word. The bend of a river, sunlight on the duct work of a manufacturing plant, ridge upon ridge of mountains — each has its moment of grace. This book could be described as a search for grace.

Two years ago I set out to photograph Virginia. I was born in Roanoke, spent my childhood in Vinton and South Boston, and have lived for the last 15 years in Charlottesville. Virginia is "home" to me.

I wanted to do something beautiful and new that would show Virginia without a layer of judgment between the subject and myself. Everything had to be looked at objectively. For me, that could be done from the air, where the view would be new and mysterious.

I was in awe when I looked at fog on the James River and photographed snow on the mountains near Monterey. Like an explorer, I was seeing places for the first time. Sights I thought were familiar became surprises. I was able to look at a chemical plant or a shipyard just as I would look at a forest covered with ice, or the falls of a river. Everything within my view was an element of a natural world.

Through the viewfinder, things would come into my vision, wave, and say, "Here I am, over here. Look at me." It could be three barns in a row, cattle in a feedlot, the exquisite flower shapes of a water treatment plant, the form of a mountain, or a parking lot full of cars. There was nothing that I deliberately set out to find. I went with a sense of discovery, of waiting for the mysterious and the new to find me.

During the two years I worked on this project, I spent over 300 hours in aircraft, exploring Virginia in every season. I flew in a dozen types of small aircraft, in helicopters, in hot-air balloons. I tried to find every aerial perspective available, from the windows of airliners to mountaintops and the roofs of tall buildings. I believe I put my eyes on every square mile of Virginia.

Flying is a dramatic way to explore. The whole process was like a mini-expedition. When weather conditions permitted a flight, we'd get out maps, decide where we were going, and when we wanted to arrive for optimal light conditions. These plans varied according to the season and the capabilities of the airplane. An aircraft adds a new dimension to photography. Along with cameras and film, suddenly there's the airplane that has its own

functions — speed and distance capabilities, fuel requirements.

The entire process was a team effort. I worked with pilot Gary Livack through most of the book. We worked together so much that I could communicate with hand motions and he would know what I meant. It was possible for me to control the airplane, even though I wasn't the pilot.

We would prepare all the equipment and number the rolls of film. An assistant would go with us to keep notes on our location and the numbers of the film I used. Then, after the film was processed, we would be able to identify locations. Even with these measures, there were so many photographs that it was difficult to know precisely where they had been made. We even tacked a flight chart up on the studio wall, drawing lines following the path of each flight we made, so we would know what areas we had explored, what remained to be done.

Things happen so fast in aerial photography that intense concentration is required. Images come by almost like a movie. It's not like having a view camera on the ground where you can study the image, move this, and refine that. In the air you can't think about the images, plan them, or adjust them. Your intuition makes you aware when a composition is about to come together. But you must learn to see quickly. Of course, you can say to the pilot, "Okay, let's go around, try it again," but you never get back to the exact spot, the same light. You have one chance.

During that period of intense concentration, there's a feeling of "lostness," when you're trying to piece an image together. You don't know if you have succeeded — you keep shooting through the whole sequence. Usually there's one frame that works. But you couldn't go up and shoot just that one frame. It's an intuitive process, not a conscious decision. I improved with experience. I could see things 20 miles away and recognize that they had possibilities, knew where the airplane needed to be, felt what the light would do, figured how much haze I could shoot through.

Change is one of the most striking phenomena of aerial photography. Within minutes the weather can change drastically. The seasons, weather conditions, and time of day seem radically different from the air. In almost every case, I went back to a location at least twice.

Lynchburg is an example. I had taken some pictures earlier in the year, but went back in the fall when the water of the James River was warm and the air was very cold. All the morning fog was lifting from the river and the city was enveloped in mist. The place was transformed. If you looked at the two photographs side by side, you wouldn't realize that they are the same place.

Sometimes finding images was like a game. One day we flew to Philpott Lake. The weather was perfect, the water was blue, and people were water skiing in the middle of the lake. We started trying to photograph them. Of course, they weren't skiing at 100 mph, the speed of the airplane. But if we started to circle, they would move past us. So Gary had a lot of fun. We had earphones, so I could talk to him. We spent 45 minutes chasing the skiers. When one would fall, we would pick up another one. We had to be aware of the lake, the water skier, our own movement, and the sunlight hitting the water. It was three-dimensional chess.

Norfolk was a fascinating area. The level of activity there is remarkable. Some places are impossible to view other than from an airplane — the coal piers, the enormous ship-building facilities. From the air you can see a giant hull becoming a ship, or miles of railroad cars loaded with coal. Then you fly off, and in five minutes, you're over the Dismal Swamp. There's so much diversity in the Tidewater area.

In contrast to the geometric patterns of the many farms of the Piedmont, Northern Virginia "explodes" away from Washington, D.C. Homes radiate from the city. These bedroom communities seemed different from homes in the Fan District of Richmond, or residences along little inlets in Norfolk, or houses clinging to the hills of Roanoke. Northern Virginia has a growing look. You fly over all these houses and suddenly there's Dulles Airport, a huge space with a futuristic look, and Tyson's Corner, a space-age community, where office buildings have satellite antennas on their roofs.

Photographing Shaffers Crossing was especially interesting because the railroad yard is a part of my earlier years with my grandfather in Vinton, just outside Roanoke. My grandfather was a station master. As a boy, I would visit him at the station and walk the rails down to the creek and cross the bridge — hundreds of times. Unconsciously, I was trying to find in the image that special feeling for the railroad that I had as a child. While making the photograph, my pilot, Gary, found flying difficult because we were shooting near the landing patterns at the Roanoke airport. He was busy getting ready to take the airplane in, talking to the tower, and I said, "No, let's go around again. Something happened back there." I was trying to catch that instant when the rails were glowing in the sun. It was just a moment, just a spot, and I was shooting with a long lens. Gary was trying to hold everything steady and stay out of air traffic. The sun was about to go down — we were running out of time. There are just a few frames, but the image I wanted found the film.

The expanse of wilderness, particularly in Southwestern Virginia and along the West Virginia border, was surprising. Photographing those areas was very tricky. It might be a beautiful day out, with a light breeze, but the mountains could be treacherous. We had to get airborne early in the morning before the ground heated. When the sun warmed the mountains, it created thermal updrafts. The turbulence wasn't necessarily dangerous, but the bouncing around was difficult on the eye and the camera. Fog was another factor. The fog in the mountains of Southwestern Virginia is absolutely beautiful, but frequently there's so much of it on the runway that you can't take off.

Sometimes as I was doing the aerial work, I could envision a photograph that I wasn't able to achieve technically. I would shoot with long lenses when thermal updrafts were shaking the airplane, or at slow shutter speeds in the low light of late afternoon, and wind up with images that almost worked but didn't.

They simply weren't sharp.

Then I heard about the camera stabilizer I now use — a device that bolts to the bottom of the camera. There are two gyroscopes, like toy tops, spinning at 19,000 rpm, one at each end, turning in opposite directions.

The stabilizer gives the camera a mind of its own. It will hold a position and resist changing it. That makes an amazing difference in the sharpness of images. The stabilizer extended the range of images I could make from the air. Traditionally, most aerial photography has been done with middle-distance lenses that record the image as you might see it from an airline window. With the stabilizer, I began to work with the full range of lenses. The very wide-angle lenses give you a feeling of this sphere, this planet. The very long lenses, up to 500 mm, see only a small part of our vision, bringing an intimacy, a closeness, to things that are far apart in reality.

This macro-, micro-view is exciting because it goes beyond the range of our eyes. Our vision conveys images to us primarily in the middle distances. There are lenses that correspond in photography — standard lenses for most cameras — that enable us to record what we see. But I try to take photography another step — to make an image that shows not only how something looks, but also how it feels. Very often paintings don't look like their subjects, and we certainly don't speak the way poetry is written. Yet people are attracted to the newness and emotion of painting and poetry. Photography can achieve those same intuitive, almost unconscious feelings.

Since I enjoy trying to extend the possibilities of photography, I tend to shoot a great deal of film in order to explore the technology, discover its capabilities. Film doesn't see a subject the way it looks to the eye through a viewfinder. I used only 35 mm cameras and the fine-grain Kodachrome 64 film which has a range of light sensitivity that isn't nearly as broad as that of our eyes. So there is always something new to learn about the film. That means filling large trash cans, but from each slide I throw away, I have learned something. It won't translate directly, but it will show up in a subtle way in the next photograph I make.

When I am able to abandon the thinking part of my mind, I can begin to make photographs. If I'm thinking, if I have something on my mind, I'm less likely to be intuitive and record grace. If you set out to explore the world about you, whether it's familiar or alien, you are given gifts. The more calm and relaxed you are, the more gifts you receive. They come back in little yellow slide boxes. Yet there's always a sense of the work never being complete. There's always more exploring to be done.

ROBERT LLEWELLYN
From an interview January 15, 1985
Charlottesville, Virginia

LAKE DRUMMOND. Virginia's largest natural lake, covering 3,200 acres, Lake Drummond lies in the heart of the Great Dismal Swamp. Surprisingly, it is the highest point in the swamp, 22.2 feet above sea level. The rest of the swamp slopes away from the shores of the lake.

FARMHOUSE, EASTERN SHORE. Each available inch of land is cultivated in this rich agricultural area, where farmers produce over 60 varieties of fruits and vegetables.

(Above and facing) RAPPAHANNOCK RIVER. The meandering Rappahannock delimits the Northern Neck of Virginia, the peninsula lying between the Rappahannock and Potomac rivers. "The Northern Neck avoids hurry; and it is, above all else, conservative," wrote Virginia satirist James Branch Cabell. "Its hazed pale atmosphere, indeed, has so soothingly inoculated the English stock which came to this part of Virginia about 1640, that few of the first settlers' descendants have left the peninsula of their own will."

CHESAPEAKE BAY BRIDGE-TUNNEL. Joining Virginia Beach-Norfolk with Virginia's Eastern Shore, the Chesapeake Bay Bridge-Tunnel crosses over and under 17.6 miles of the Chesapeake Bay where it meets the Atlantic Ocean. The three bridges of the construction are joined by two tunnels, each nearly a mile long, which rest on man-made islands dredged from the bottom of the bay.

(Facing) BOATHOUSE, EASTERN SHORE. The Chesapeake Bay has 4,600 miles of shoreline and is the largest estuary in the eastern United States. It is also one of the best fishing areas in the world. Chesapeake's famed "watermen" have taken fish, crabs, clams, and oysters from the waters and flats of the bay for generations.

FISHING BOATS, FLEETON. Located in Northumberland County, Fleeton earns much of its livelihood from Chesapeake Bay. In addition to shellfish, seafoods taken from the bay include croakers, flounders, menhaden, sea bass, striped bass, and sea trout.

(*Above and facing*) TANGIER ISLAND. Captain John Smith named this tiny island near the mouth of the Potomac River when he explored the area in 1607. Appropriately, many of its inhabitants still speak with an Elizabethan accent. There are no automobiles on the island. Residents travel by bicycle and boat. In the War of 1812, British troops impressed into service the young males on Tangier to attack the city of Baltimore. But the women of the island sank all the small vessels essential to the campaign, thus saving their men.

GOVERNOR'S PALACE, WILLIAMSBURG. Royal Governor Alexander Spotswood oversaw the building of the Governor's Palace in 1720. The structure included a ballroom wing and formal garden and served as the residence of seven colonial governors. Patrick Henry and Thomas Jefferson, the first two governors of the Commonwealth during the Revolutionary War, also resided in the mansion.

TRENCHES, YORKTOWN. Six years after the victory he had won over Lord Cornwallis at Yorktown in 1781, George Washington wrote, "The disadvantageous circumstances on our part, under which the war was undertaken, can never be forgotten. The singular interpositions of Providence in our feeble condition were such, as could scarcely escape the attention of the most unobserving; while the unparalleled perseverance of the Armies of the U. States, through almost every possible suffering and discouragement for the space of eight long years, was little short of a standing miracle."

(Pages 26-27, overleaf) NORFOLK. Located on the site of an Indian town called Skicoak, Norfolk was founded by decree of King Charles II on August 16, 1682. During the Revolutionary War, the warships of Lord Dunmore bombarded Norfolk, and British sailors came ashore and set fire to the city's warehouses. The colonials, fearing that they would not be able to hold the city, set the remaining dwellings on fire. Norfolk was burned to the ground.

NORFOLK INTERNATIONAL TERMINAL. At this container-ship terminal, fully loaded truck trailers are placed directly on board cargo ships.

COLLIERS, HAMPTON ROADS. In the War of 1812, British naval forces entered the Chesapeake Bay, pillaged Hampton, and sailed up the Potomac River to attack Washington. The capital city was captured on August 24, 1814. President and Mrs. Madison fled into the Virginia countryside to escape capture. To prevent the recurrence of such an event, Congress authorized the building of a dozen coastal forts during President Monroe's administration. Fortress Monroe still guards the entrance to Hampton Roads.

(Above and facing) NEWPORT NEWS SHIPBUILDING AND DRY DOCK COMPANY. Situated on Hampton Roads, one of the world's largest natural harbors, Newport News Shipbuilding was organized in 1885 by Collis P. Huntington, an entrepreneur who began his business career as a 16-year-old traveling salesman and went on to shape a transportation and manufacturing empire. The shipyard has produced the 990-foot passenger liner *United States* and the massive nuclear-powered aircraft carrier, the U. S. S. *Nimitz*.

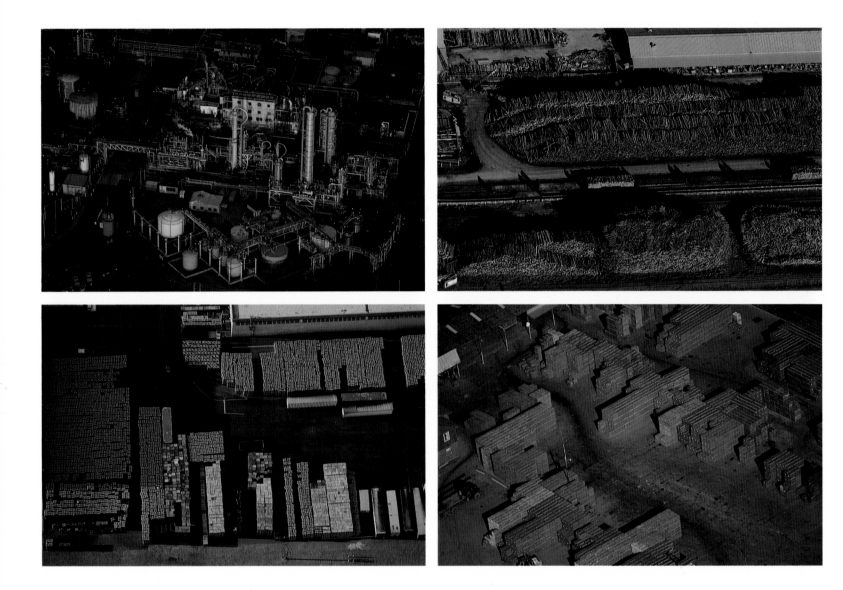

INDUSTRY BEGAN IN VIRGINIA IN 1608 with the establishment of a glass factory in Jamestown. Diverse production facilities are found throughout the state today. (*Clockwise, from upper left*) Allied Corporation, Fibers Division, is located in Hopewell. Union Camp Corporation, near Franklin, began in 1887 when six Camp brothers undertook logging operations in Southside Virginia. Webster Brick Company is located near Somerset in Orange County. The company produces brick made from shale mined on the property. Anheuser-Busch Brewery, near Williamsburg, is next door to the "Old Country", Busch Gardens, where visitors may enjoy a variety of amusements, including a visit to the stables of the Anheuser-Busch Clydesdales.

(*Facing*) RAILROAD CARS, NORFOLK. Among the extraordinary features of Norfolk harbor is the Norfolk Southern Corporation's coal-loading dock, which can berth four colliers simultaneously. The yards surrounding the dock can hold 11,520 coal hopper railroad cars.

(Facing) "WATERSIDE", NORFOLK. A public market and festival place, Waterside features produce and retail vendors.

U. S. NAVY SUBMARINES AND SHIPS, NORFOLK. Two Virginians changed the course of naval history. During the Civil War, master engineers John L. Porter, of Portsmouth, and John Mercer Brooke, of Lexington, designed the ironclad, *Virginia*, better known as the *Merrimac*. In an engagement with Union battleships at Hampton Roads, March 8, 1862, the Confederate ironclad demonstrated the superiority of armored warships.

(Facing) VIRGINIA BEACH. Offering eight miles of sand and ocean to any visitor, Virginia Beach attracts about 2 million tourists each year. Nearby is Cape Henry, where the small band of English settlers who would found Jamestown first landed on April 26, 1607.

AIRCRAFT CARRIERS, NORFOLK. The Norfolk Naval Station and Naval Air Station is the largest naval installation in the world, home port for some 118 ships of the Atlantic and Mediterranean Fleets, 32 aircraft squadrons, and 65 shore activities. The naval base is also headquarters for SACLANT, Supreme Allied Command Atlantic, Western Arm of NATO.

(Pages 38-39, overleaf) SUNBATHERS, VIRGINIA BEACH. "The sun rejoices in his strength, dazzling and burning, and yet, to me, never unpleasantly weakening," wrote poet Walt Whitman, who lived in Virginia for over a year. "It is not the panting tropical heat, but invigorates."

JAMES RIVER, RICHMOND. Captains Christopher Newport, John Smith, Gabriel Archer, and 21 adventurers reached the falls of the James River on May 23, 1607, only 10 days after landing at Jamestown. They had reached the site of modern Richmond.

(*Above and facing*) JAMES RIVER, RICHMOND. Just as British sailing vessels navigated the river during the 17th century, modern cargo ships, tugs, and barges still ply their trade on the James River. With its deep channel and canals, the James at Richmond is navigable for ocean-going vessels. The city is a United States Customs Port of Entry.

CAPITOL, RICHMOND. Designed by Thomas Jefferson, the building is patterned after the Maison Carée in Nîmes, France. Houdon's statue of George Washington in military dress stands in the rotunda of the Capitol. In its courtroom, Aaron Burr was tried for treason, with John Marshall presiding. The Congress of the Confederacy met in the building, 1861-65. Robert E. Lee received his sword as Commander of the Army of Virginia at the Capitol, and the body of "Stonewall" Jackson lay in state there after he was mortally wounded at Chancellorsville.

RICHMOND. Capital of Virginia since 1779 and a vigorous financial and industrial center, Richmond has endured the destruction of two wars. Benedict Arnold and British troops raided the city in 1781. As Capital of the Confederacy, the city was nearly leveled by bombardment and fire.

HOLLYWOOD CEMETERY, RICHMOND. Named for its magnificent holly trees, the cemetery is the resting place of U. S. Presidents James Monroe and John Tyler, Confederate President Jefferson Davis, General J. E. B. Stuart, and 18,000 Confederate soldiers. Virginia writers Ellen Glasgow and James Branch Cabell are also buried there.

(Pages 48-49, overleaf) MONTICELLO. Thomas Jefferson spent over 40 years building his home, Monticello, on his "little mountain" outside Charlottesville. Jefferson returned to the estate following his Presidency. "I am retired to Monticello," he wrote his friend, General Thaddeus Kosciusko, in 1810, "where, in the bosom of my family, and surrounded by my books, I enjoy a repose to which I have been long a stranger."

UNIVERSITY OF VIRGINIA, CHARLOTTESVILLE. Thomas Jefferson undertook the architectural drawings for the University when he was 73 years old, supervised the construction of its first building, and hired the University's first faculty. He patterned his Rotunda, the central building of "the Lawn", after the classical Roman Pantheon. The University is recognized as one of the country's finest architectural achievements.

MONTPELIER, NEAR ORANGE. Montpelier is the family estate of President James Madison. Known as the "Father of the Constitution," Madison planned the system of checks and balances among the judicial, legislative, and executive branches of government. Madison died at Montpelier on June 28, 1836, and is buried in a family plot nearby.

HORSE FARM, ALBEMARLE COUNTY. "In the breast of every Virginian, if he was not so fortunate as to inherit, or expect to inherit, such a plantation," wrote land baron and horse breeder John Randolph of Roanoke, "was the resolve to realize his ideal of perfect felicity by sooner or later buying one and spending the remainder of his days on it in the enjoyment of the rural pleasures, which are among the few human pleasures that leave no bitter taste in the mouth."

(*Facing*) HORSES, ALBEMARLE COUNTY. "The Virginians, of all ranks and denominations, are excessively fond of horses, and especially those of the race breed," wrote John F. S. Smyth in 1769. "Nobody walks on foot the smallest distance, except when hunting; indeed, a man will frequently go five miles to catch a horse, to ride only one mile afterwards."

TRUCK SPREADING LIME, NEAR GORDONSVILLE. Farming in Virginia is over 400 years old. Native Algonquin tribesmen acquainted the English colonials with some of their indigenous agricultural products, including maize, tobacco, and yams.

BARBOURSVILLE VINEYARD. Thomas Jefferson was one of the first
Virginians to experiment with viticulture. He imported a number of
European vines after a personal tour of vineyards in France and Germany.
While there is no record that Jefferson's efforts met with success, modern
grafting and spraying techniques have led to a flourishing wine industry in
the Commonwealth, where Riesling, Cabernet Sauvignon, Gewurtztraminer,
Merlot, Chardonnay, and Rosé varietals are grown today.

HAYBALES, NEAR CHARLOTTESVILLE. A significant development in modern agriculture was the invention of the mechanical reaper by Virginian Cyrus McCormick. He described his invention in an 1839 advertisement: "The subscriber, in consequence of other engagements and a failure in the crops of grain, has done nothing with this machine for several years, until recently, since which he has made some important improvements upon it. He has cut with it during the present harvest about 75 acres of Wheat and Rye, and thinks its performance now unexceptionable. It will cut one and a half to two acres an hour, with two horses and two hands, leaving the grain in sheaves, ready for tying, and will cut and save the grain much cleaner than the ordinary mode of cradling whether it be tangled or straight. The machine is not complicated or liable to get out of order—but is essentially durable, and will cost about $50."

(*Facing*) FAUQUIER COUNTY. Misty fields in this section of Virginia often resound with the baying of fox hounds and the pounding of horses' hooves. "The hunt" is a Virginia tradition, popular from the days when George Washington was a young man.

CATTLE FARM, NEAR CULPEPER. Most of the self-sufficient plantations
and homesteads that characterized Virginia agriculture for hundreds of years
have given way to more commercial operations, which make use of heavy
machinery and sophisticated business planning.

SOW AND PIGS. The first recorded shipment of Southside Virginia's famous Smithfield ham was in 1779. The hickory-smoked hams are said to receive their distinctive flavor from the peanuts, or "goobers," the hogs are fed.

(Pages 60-61, overleaf) FARM, NEAR GORDONSVILLE. In this agricultural region Zachary Taylor, 12th President of the United States, was born on November 24, 1784. Virginia is the native state of seven other Presidents: George Washington, Thomas Jefferson, James Madison, James Monroe, William Henry Harrison, John Tyler, and Woodrow Wilson.

FIELD, ALBEMARLE COUNTY. "Dilapidated, fenceless, and trodden with war as Virginia is," wrote poet Walt Whitman in 1882, "wherever I move across her surface, I find myself rous'd to surprise and admiration. What capacity for products, improvements, human life, nourishment and expansion....The soil is yet far above the average of any of the northern States. And how full of breadth the scenery, everywhere distant mountains, everywhere convenient rivers."

INGLECRESS HORSE FARM, ALBEMARLE COUNTY. A number of farms in Virginia are known for their thoroughbred racehorses. One of the Commonwealth's most famous sons, Secretariat, winner of horse racing's Triple Crown, makes his home at "The Meadow", a thoroughbred horse farm in Caroline County.

LYNCHBURG. After 17-year-old John Lynch established a ferry that replaced a difficult ford on the James River in 1757, others built dwellings on the navigable river near his ferry house. "Lynchburg" grew into a center for the tobacco trade. At Riverside Park is the hull of the packet boat "Marshall", which carried the remains of "Stonewall" Jackson to Lexington after his death at Chancellorsville. The "Marshall" was the last of the steam packets which for years provided the principal means of transportation along the James River and Kanawha Canal.

64

SCHOOL BUS, NEAR BOSWELL'S TAVERN. Free education in Virginia had its beginnings soon after the founding of Jamestown. In addition to the Syms Free School, founded in 1634, and the Eaton Free School, established a few years later, there were seven other early institutions generally known as "parish schools". The Syms and Eaton schools were the first free schools in America.

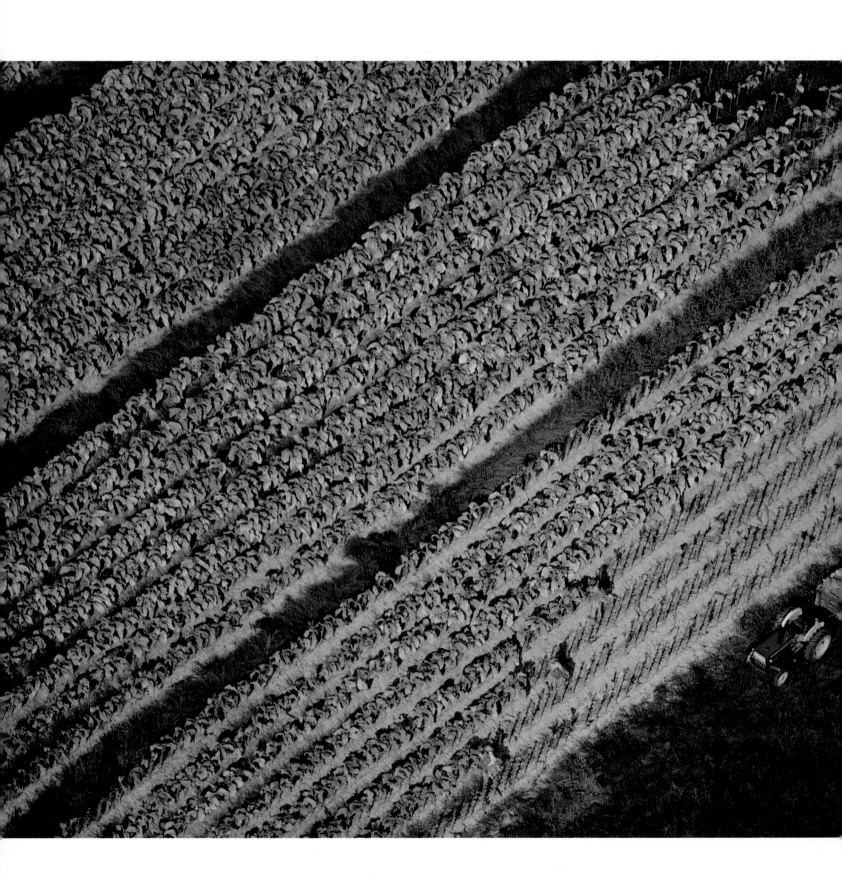

PRINCE EDWARD COUNTY. Harvest in this tobacco field near Farmville is a reminder of the days when tobacco, the "joviall weed," was the gold of Virginia commerce. Initiated by colonial planter John Rolfe, who would later marry the Algonquin princess Pocahontas, the tobacco trade became a staple of Britain's expanding imperial economy and remained so for 200 years.

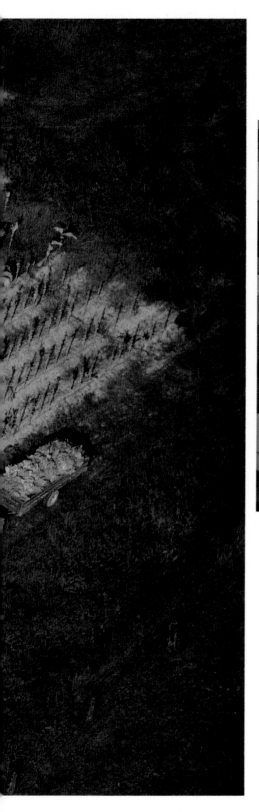

TOBACCO WAREHOUSES, DANVILLE. Danville has nine tobacco auction warehouses with 1.8 million square feet of space and 58 storage warehouses with a capacity of 370 million pounds of tobacco. Farmers bring baskets of tobacco to be weighed and graded. Buyers trail an auctioneer along rows of graded baskets, which are sold individually in a matter of seconds. Danville is the largest center for tobacco sales in Virginia.

ORANGE COUNTY. "There are people who would leave Paradise to go to Orange County," wrote Virginian George Bagby, editor of the *Southern Literary Messenger*, shortly before the Civil War, "and I am one of them."

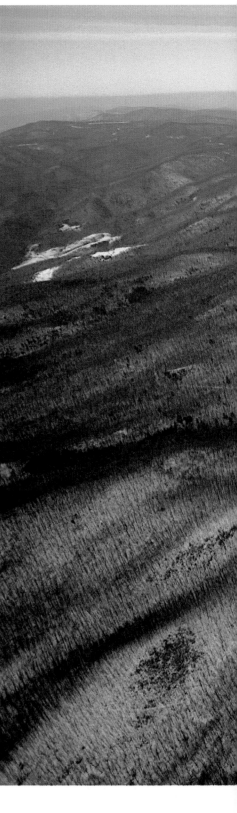

(*Pages 70-71, overleaf*) BLUE RIDGE MOUNTAINS. Woodrow Wilson, a native of Staunton, which lies just west of the Blue Ridge, returned in 1912 for a birthday party given for him by the townspeople. "Men believe now that sooner or later their wrongs are going to be righted, and that a time is going to dawn when justice will be the average and usual thing in the administration of human affairs," Wilson said. "You may imagine the pleasure, therefore, that it gives me to come back to the place where these standards cannot be questioned, for these standards were first established, so far as this side of the water is concerned, in Virginia. And no Virginian can stand up and look the history of Virginia in the face and doubt what the future is going to be....all that is needed is momentum. It does not need any cunning tongue. It does not need eloquence. It just needs the kind of serenity which enables you to steer by the stars and not the ground."

WINCHESTER. Once the camping ground for Shawnee war parties, Winchester was settled by Quakers in 1732. It was the site of six battles during the Civil War; the city changed flags 70 times in the course of that conflict. The many orchards surrounding the city have made it the center of the Shenandoah Valley Apple Blossom Festival held each spring.

BLUE RIDGE PARKWAY, NEAR WAYNESBORO. Established in 1936, the Blue Ridge Parkway was the first recreational area of the National Park System. Two hundred seventeen miles of the Parkway are in Virginia. The roadway follows the crest of the Blue Ridge Mountains at an average altitude of 3,000 feet.

(Above and facing) WINTERGREEN, NELSON COUNTY. A 10,000-acre resort located in the Blue Ridge Mountains near the Blue Ridge Parkway and the Skyline Drive, Wintergreen features modern snow-making equipment and a variety of ski slopes.

(Above and facing) KERR RESERVOIR, NEAR CLARKSVILLE. In August 1940, torrential rains flooded croplands along the Roanoke River, its 30th severe flood since the Civil War. Representative John H. Kerr of the Second Congressional District of North Carolina argued that the Roanoke River had to be controlled. The result was the John H. Kerr Dam and Reservoir, whose waters spread into both Virginia and North Carolina. Some staunch Virginians insist on calling the impoundment the Buggs Island Dam and Reservoir, naming it for an island lying below the dam on the Virginia side.

PHILPOTT LAKE. Twelve miles northwest of Martinsville is the Smith
River dam that forms Philpott Lake. The 2,880-acre reservoir is surrounded
by the lower slopes of the Blue Ridge Mountains.

JAMES RIVER "TUBERS," NEAR SCOTTSVILLE. Riding inner tubes on the James is a refreshing warm-weather activity in central Virginia. Tubers park their vehicles in Scottsville and are taken upstream for a leisurely, three-mile float back to Hatton's Ferry Landing, built in 1890.

(Above and facing) FOOTBALL TEAM AND CARNIVAL, MARTINSVILLE.
Frontiersman and state militia brigadier general Joseph Martin founded
Martinsville in 1791. Martin was a remarkably colorful man. Over six feet
tall, brawny, the father of 18 children, he wore buckled knee breeches and
a great beard that he braided and thrust inside his shirt. In all likelihood
he would be at home both on the modern gridiron or at a carnival sideshow.

(Pages 82-83, overleaf) MOUNTAINS, NEAR MONTEREY. Highland County's mountain peaks lie within two national forests, the George Washington National Forest to the east, and the Monongahela National Forest to the west. Monterey, the county seat, serves as headquarters for the annual Highland Maple Festival, held in March.

SHENANDOAH VALLEY. Recognized as one of the great agricultural areas of Virginia since it was settled in the 18th century, the Shenandoah Valley is the cradle of a hardy upland culture that produced Texas statesman Sam Houston, inventor Cyrus McCormick, Confederate General "Stonewall" Jackson, and President Woodrow Wilson. The valley was called "the Granary of the Confederacy" because of the strategic importance of its crops during the Civil War. After his forces had ravaged the land, Federal cavalry officer Philip Sheridan reported that "a crow couldn't fly across the Valley of Virginia without a pack of rations on his back."

SHENANDOAH VALLEY. "Those who labour in the earth are the chosen people of God, if ever he had a chosen people, whose breasts he has made his peculiar deposit for substantial and genuine virtue," wrote Thomas Jefferson. "It is the focus in which he keeps alive that sacred fire, which otherwise might escape from the face of the earth. Corruption of morals in the mass of cultivators is a phenomenon of which no age nor nation has furnished an example."

TURKEY FARM, ROCKINGHAM COUNTY. Located in the Shenandoah Valley, 868-square-mile Rockingham County is one of the major turkey-producing areas in the United States.

INTERSTATE 81, SHENANDOAH VALLEY. Following the Valley of Virginia from Winchester in the north to Bristol in the mountains of the southwest, I-81, a major corridor for interstate trucking, spans the Commonwealth.

(Pages 88-89, overleaf) ROANOKE. A young city by Tidewater Virginia standards, Roanoke took its name in 1882 after two railroads—the Norfolk and Western and the Shenandoah Valley—built a junction at the frontier settlement then called Big Lick. The area was an ancient hunting ground. Game was drawn to the nearby mineral and salt deposits, or "licks". Roanoke today is an industrial, financial, and transportation center.

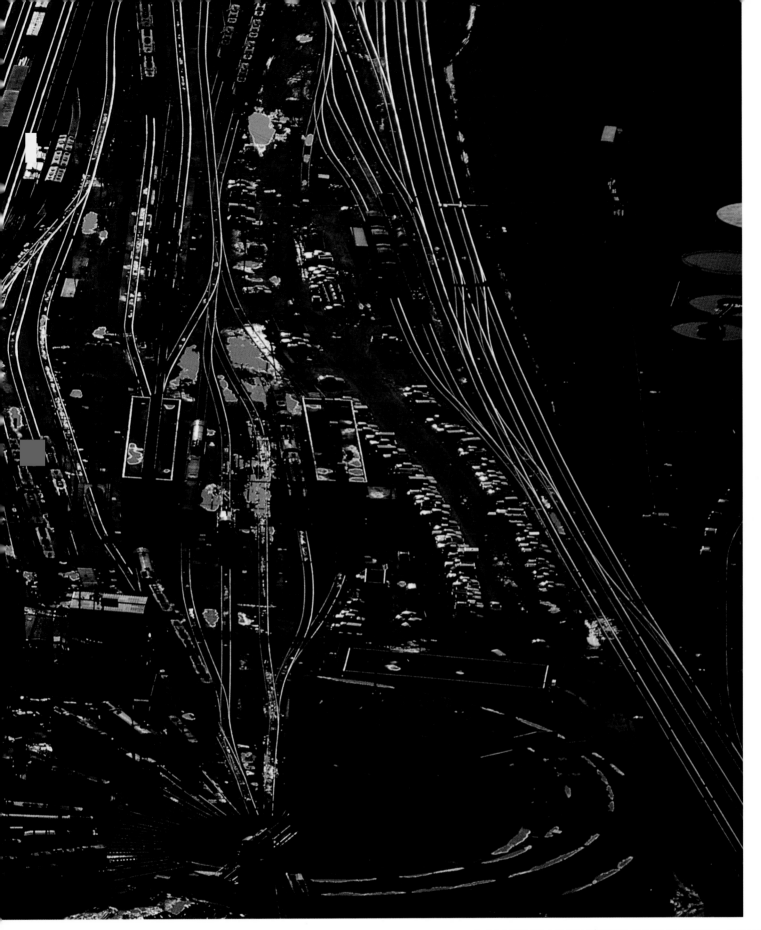

SHAFFERS CROSSING LOCOMOTIVE ROUNDHOUSE, ROANOKE. The first buildings for this Norfolk Southern Corporation locomotive maintenance and repair facility were constructed in 1919. The 40-stall round-house with its 115-foot turntable provided service for steam locomotives built at the Norfolk and Western Railway "Shops" in Roanoke, and was recognized as one of the leading steam locomotive maintenance and repair facilities in the country. In 1955 Shaffers Crossing was converted to diesel locomotive service, and in 1984, the roundhouse itself was replaced by a modern service facility.

WOODS, NEAR MANASSAS. The first Battle of Manassas in 1861 fore-
told the protracted and bloody war that would follow. It also earned
Confederate General Thomas Jonathan Jackson his famous nickname.
"There stands Jackson like a stone wall," exclaimed General B. E. Bee
during the battle. "Rally behind the Virginians!"

BURIAL, NEAR LEXINGTON. "We came equal into the world, and equal we shall go out of it," wrote George Mason, author of the Virginia Bill of Rights, in 1774. "All men are by nature born equally free and independent....In all our associations, in all our agreements, let us never lose sight of this fundamental maxim — that all power was originally lodged in and consequently is derived from the people."

(Pages 94-95, overleaf) VALLEYS, NEAR CLINCH MOUNTAINS. Under Virginia's original charter, its mountains opened upon an empire that extended to the Pacific Ocean. All or part of eight other states — Illinois, Indiana, Kentucky, Michigan, Minnesota, Ohio, West Virginia, and Wisconsin — were formed from land originally claimed by Virginia. The state's western border extends to Cumberland Gap, which is 25 miles west of the meridian on which Detroit, Michigan lies.

STRIP MINE, WISE COUNTY. Large reserves of coal are found in the mountains of western Virginia. Massive earth-moving equipment is used to remove the coal, which is most often transported by rail from the region. Rotary dump mechanisms capable of unloading a 155-ton railroad car by turning it upside down are found at some stations.

(Facing) FARM AND FAMILY CEMETERY, FLOYD COUNTY. This mountainous county is named for John Floyd, Governor of Virginia when the county was formed in 1831. In its earth lie the remains of the sturdy people who carved homesteads from the land two centuries ago. Many of their descendants still farm the land. Also buried there is Annie Maria Smith, a New England school teacher who lived for a time in Richmond. Her friendship with Edgar Allan Poe was given lasting expression in his poem, "For Annie".

TREE AND HAYBALES, BURKE'S GARDEN. Much bluegrass grows in this limestone bowl near the Brushy Mountains. Virginia lay under water 600 million years ago, when marine life deposited the limestone beneath its soil. Folding and faulting during the Ordovician Period of the Paleozoic Era thrust the mountain structure from the seabed.

WOODLANDS, SOUTHWESTERN VIRGINIA. A wide variety of trees can be found from the Tidewater section of the Commonwealth to the mountains. There are 12 types of oak, five varieties of pine, three kinds of cedar, maple, birch, and elm, and two types of walnut, locust, gum, and poplar. Other species include cypress, basswood, ash, hickory, persimmon, beech, holly, sycamore, redbud, hemlock, and, of course, dogwood.

HERCULES, INC., PULASKI. Iron oxide pigment is manufactured in this large facility near Pulaski. The town is named in honor of Count Casimir Pulaski, a Polish patriot who fought with American forces in the Revolutionary War.

RADFORD ARMY AMMUNITION PLANT, NEAR DUBLIN. Underground "igloos" are used to store propellants and explosives produced at the Hercules, Inc. plant. Built in 1941, the bunkers serve to minimize the possibility of an explosion.

(*Pages 102-103, overleaf*) TOBACCO HARVEST, WISE COUNTY. Stream valleys and hillcrests provide level farmland in mountainous southwestern Virginia. In this area is Mt. Rogers, the highest point in Virginia—5,729 feet above sea level. Burley tobacco is grown extensively in a few counties in this region.

GREAT FALLS, POTOMAC RIVER. A spectacular natural area, the Great
Falls are within 15 miles of the White House in Washington, D.C. The
Potomac River drops 77 feet in less than three-quarters of a mile.

ROTUNDA, TYSON'S CORNER SHOPPING CENTER. Tyson's Corner stands on Route 7, one of the oldest and most important roads in Fairfax County. Beginning in Alexandria and running west to Winchester and a junction with the Philadelphia Wagon Road, the route was often used by the young surveyor, George Washington, on journeys to the frontier. The area was still rural when Tyson's Corner Shopping Center was built in 1968.

KEY BRIDGE. Named for Francis Scott Key, the bridge spans the Potomac River from Virginia to Georgetown. Completed in 1923, Key Bridge has been modified many times. It stands near the site of Aqueduct Bridge, which dates from 1843. Aqueduct Bridge included a wooden flume for canal boats and a plank bridge for vehicles and livestock. Its old masonry piers still stand in the river, serving as ice baffles for bridges downstream.

POTOMAC RIVER. Near Quantico the hulls of a number of sunken vessels are visible in the river. These wooden barges and freighters were built as an emergency measure during World War I, but were not completed until the war had nearly ended. Purchased by a private contractor, the vessels were never resold. Eventually the Potomac claimed them.

RESTON. The first effort in the United States to create a fully planned community near a major urban center, Reston is a full-scale, self-contained city. Thirty-acre Lake Anne is a part of the city, whose master plan designates 45 percent of usable space for public purposes, including schools, parks, roads, trails, walkways, churches, golf courses, swimming pools, tennis courts, and malls.

TYSON'S CORNER. In 1811, Richard Bland Lee, a founder of the city of Washington and Northern Virginia's first representative to Congress, moved with his wife Elizabeth to "Strawberry Vale." Around his unpretentious estate in the hilly countryside grew the suburb of Tyson's Corner. About 1960, Bland's farmhouse at Strawberry Vale was demolished to provide space for an access ramp to the beltway around Washington.

WOODLANDS ON RAPIDAN RIVER, NEAR CHANCELLORSVILLE.
Mortally wounded by his own troops following the Battle of Chancellorsville in 1863, "Stonewall" Jackson uttered his final command, "We will
cross the river and rest in the shade of the trees."

(Pages 112-113, overleaf) ARLINGTON NATIONAL CEMETERY. The first two soldier-dead were interred in Arlington National Cemetery on May 13, 1864. One month later, on June 15, Edwin M. Stanton, President Abraham Lincoln's Secretary of War, formally designated Arlington as a military cemetery for the burial of soldiers from hospitals in the area. The land derived from Arlington estate, home of the George Washington Parke Custis and Robert E. Lee families.

U. S. MARINE CORPS IWO JIMA MEMORIAL. The statue is located in Arlington, a tract of land ceded to the District of Columbia, but restored to Virginia in 1847. A tribute to the raising of the American flag over Mt. Suribachi in 1945, the Marine Corps Memorial is the largest bronze cast statue in the world.

MOUNT VERNON. South of Alexandria on the Potomac River, Mount Vernon was George Washington's home, 1754-99. Washington more than doubled the size of the house he originally inherited. To support the activities of the mansion, he built a village-like group of "dependencies," or service buildings. The gardens of the house remain substantially as they were during Washington's lifetime.

(Facing) GEORGE WASHINGTON MASONIC NATIONAL MEMORIAL, ALEXANDRIA. The monument is a gift of the Freemasons of the United States to honor the memory of George Washington, who was a member. Standing on Shooter's Hill, the memorial is 331 feet tall. Young Washington helped survey the streets of Alexandria, one of Virginia's oldest cities, in 1749.

PENTAGON. A five-sided colossus in Arlington, just across the Potomac River from Washington, D.C., the Pentagon was built in 1941-43. With 17.5 miles of corridors, roughly the length of the Chesapeake Bay Bridge-Tunnel, it is the largest office building in the world.

(Pages 118-119, overleaf) POTOMAC RIVER. The southern bank of the Potomac is the northern boundary of Virginia. One meaning given "Potomac" is "River of Swans." The river received its name from John Smith, who in 1608 found an Indian "King's House" named "Patawomack" near the stream. In the Algonquin language, the word means "where something is brought", probably denoting the use of the river as a trading place long before the English arrived.

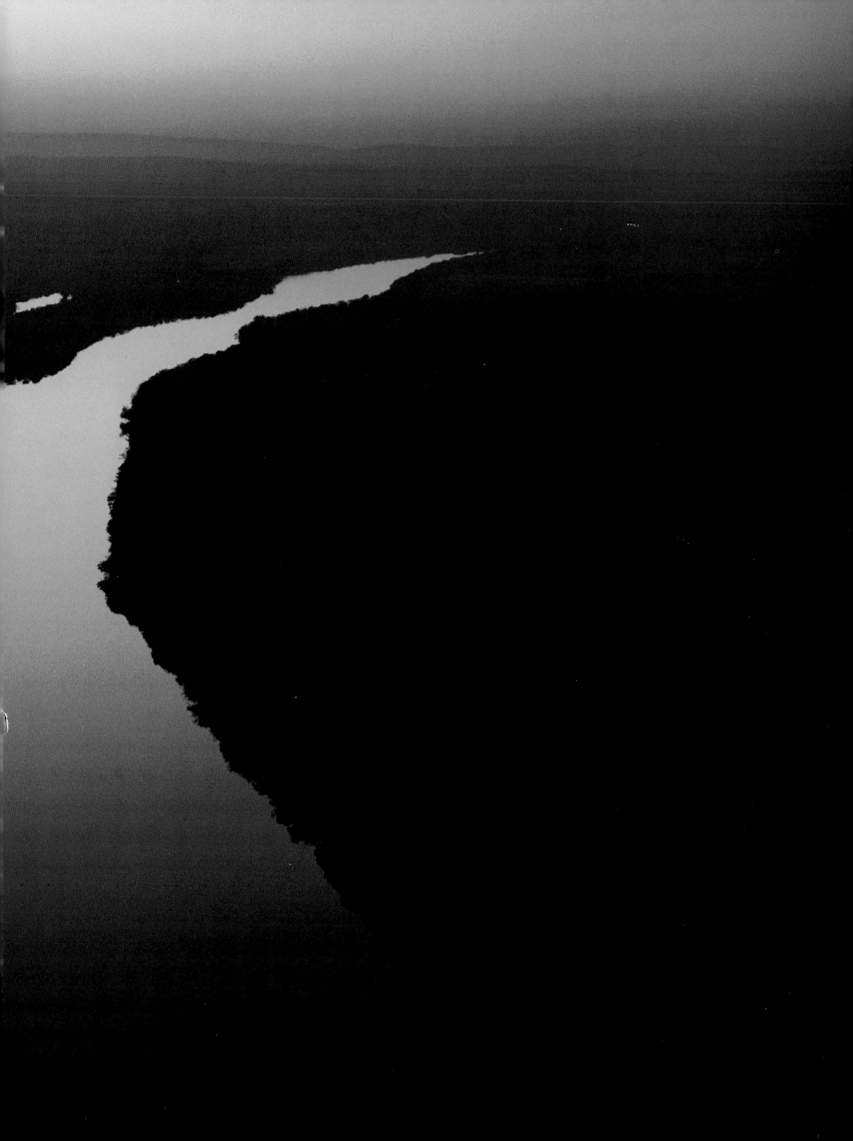

This book is for my grandmother,
Bessie Terry Kent, who has always been fond of Virginia and interested in photography, and bought
me my first camera when I was 12.
Although 88 years old, she often went flying with us when we were near her Vinton home.

Gary Livack, of Arlington, a good friend and excellent pilot,
contributed his time, skill, and enthusiasm to this project. Aeronaut Rick Behr offered his Boar's Head
hot-air balloon for many of the low-altitude aerial photographs.
David Miller, of Falls Church, helped chart many of the locations on extended flights.
Production and editing were assisted by Kathy Thomas
and Lindsay Eckford. My wife, Bobbi, contributed to all phases of this book, and was always
a source of support.

ROBERT LLEWELLYN